The First Baby Food Cookbook

Melinda Morris

Illustrated by Anke van Dun

GROSSET & DUNLAP
A FILMWAYS COMPANY
Publishers • New York

*With love and appreciation
to my husband, Roger Stephens*

Introduction

THE FIRST BABYFOOD COOKBOOK offers a wide variety of nutritious, appealing foods that range from meals you can whip up for the baby in seconds to suggestions for taking what the rest of the family is eating and adapting it to the baby's needs. The recipes are arranged from the fairly simple, for those just beginning to eat solid food, to dishes that a fifteen-month-old will enjoy. In addition, hints are included as to how to use leftovers!

Of course, the age when a baby is ready for specific foods and combinations of foods varies slightly. For example, most pediatricians will advise you not to give your baby eggs until he is around six months old as they have been known to cause allergies in some infants. *So be sure to check with your doctor before serving your baby a new food for the first time.*

When I was a baby I ate the standard breakfast foods: cereal, fruit, bacon, ham and eggs. Today more and more pediatricians are recommending a wide, exciting variety of foods including soups, fish, fruit breads, fruit desserts, and even such sophisticated fare as Quiche Lorraine for your baby's breakfast. And why not! Breakfast should be something your baby eagerly looks forward to—a meal full of special nourishing treats to help him start the day off feeling well.

Contents

FRUIT

Most four-to-six-week-old babies enjoy all fruits with the exception of the citrus variety to which young babies have been known to develop allergies. However, by the time they are six months old most babies are able to drink orange as well as all other citrus juices with no complications.

Make sure you wash fruit thoroughly in addition to removing all seeds and pits. The preparation of individual fruits is discussed in this section.

Peach
Wash thoroughly and remove pit. Peel, then blend with 1 tablespoon water until smooth.

Banana
Peel banana. Cut in half, mash and serve 1/2 banana at a time.

Pear
Halve pear, remove seeds and peel. Cut into chunks and blend thoroughly with 1 tablespoon water.

Apple
Halve apple, remove seeds and peel. Cut into chunks and blend thoroughly with 4 tablespoons water. (For applesauce flavor you may want to add 1 teaspoon granulated sugar and 1/2 teaspoon brown sugar.)

Prunes (Bulk)
Let prunes soak in hot water (2 1/4 cups to each 1/2 pound) for 2 hours. Then cook slowly in same water until prunes become plump and tender. Remove pits, blend until smooth and serve. When using packaged prunes follow directions on package.

Pineapple
Cut chunks from a fresh pineapple. Either crush thoroughly with a fork or blend until smooth. If pineapple is not particularly juicy, add a tablespoon or two of water.

Apricot
Wash thoroughly and remove pit. Peel and blend with 1 tablespoon water until smooth.

Avocado
Cut avocado in half, then peel and pit. Mash about 1/8 cup avocado and serve.

Raspberries
Stem 6 raspberries. Wash thoroughly, blend with 1/2 teaspoon sugar, 2 tablespoons water and serve.

Strawberries
Stem 6 strawberries. Wash thoroughly, mash and serve.

Orange Juice
There is no need to buy the expensive orange juice made especially for babies. Fresh orange juice is best of all—just squeeze oranges, strain and serve.

SOUPS

One of the nice things about homemade soup —aside even from its superior taste—is that the same soup can serve not only the baby but the rest of the family as well. Make it in large enough quantities and you can freeze whatever is left over for future use.

Chicken Noodle Soup
(Serves 6)

4 cups chicken broth
1 1/4 cups cooked egg noodles
1 cup cooked chicken, boned

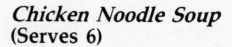

Blend broth, noodles and chicken together. Let simmer in a saucepan for about 20 minutes before serving.

This is an ideal "first soup" to give your baby and tends to be a perennial favorite among young children as well.

Cream of Tomato Soup
(Serves 4-6)

4 fresh tomatoes
4 cups milk

Peel tomatoes and blend with milk. Heat in a saucepan for about 10 minutes and serve.

For the citrus-fruit lovers in your family, add 1/8-inch slice orange to each bowl of soup.

Cream of Mushroom Soup (Serves 4-6)

1/4 cup very finely chopped mushrooms
1 1/2 cups milk
3 tablespoons butter
1 tablespoon flour
1 cup chicken broth

Blend mushrooms and 1/2 cup milk together thoroughly. In a saucepan melt butter, then add mushroom mixture. Cook slowly for about 10 minutes. Stir in flour and add chicken broth and 1 cup milk. Cook slowly for 5 more minutes and serve.

A generous sprinkling of coarsely ground black pepper will heighten the flavor of your family's soup.

Vegetable Soup
(Serves 4-6)

4 tablespoons butter
1 potato, diced
2 carrots, sliced
1/4 pound string beans, sliced
1/2 pound green peas, shelled
1/2 pound spinach, washed and dried
4 cups chicken broth
1/2 cup milk

Melt butter in a saucepan. Add all the vegetables and chicken broth. Bring to a boil. Let simmer over low heat for 25 minutes. Then mix in blender for 5 or 6 seconds and pour back into pan. Stir in milk, reheat and serve.

If you have a garden, try growing some of your own vegetables. You can't beat the home-grown variety for freshness!

Fruit Soup
(Serves 4-6)

2 pears
4 apricots
3 peaches
3 cups milk

Prepare fruits (according to directions in fruit section). Blend thoroughly with milk, heat for about 10 minutes and serve.

This is a soup which also tastes good served cold.

Cream of Celery Soup (Serves 4-5)

2 cups diced celery
3 tablespoons butter
1 tablespoon flour
3 egg yolks
2 1/2 cups milk

Boil celery in about 4 inches water for 20 minutes. Drain, then mix thoroughly in blender.

Next, blend butter and flour in a pan over low heat. When mixture begins to thicken, stir in egg yolks, milk and celery. Let simmer for 30 minutes before serving.

Add diced chicken and egg noodles to any leftover soup and you'll have a delicious-tasting casserole.

Pea Soup
(Serves 4-5)

2 pounds green peas
3 egg yolks
2 cups milk
1 cup water

Shell peas and boil in about 4 inches water for 8 minutes. Drain water from peas. Pour peas into blender and mix thoroughly. Add egg yolks, milk and water. Blend for about 30 seconds. Pour into a pan and let simmer for 35 minutes before serving.

After you have set aside your baby's portion of soup, use the rest in a curried pea soup for the other members of your family. Stir in 2 tablespoons curry powder, simmer for 5 minutes and serve.

Cream of Asparagus Soup (Serves 4-6)

1 pound fresh asparagus
3 tablespoons butter
1 tablespoon flour
1 cup milk
2 cups chicken broth
2 egg yolks

Cook asparagus in about 3 inches water for 15 minutes. In another pan, blend butter and flour over low heat. Add milk and stir. When mixture begins to thicken, add broth and let simmer for 2-3 minutes.

Drain cooked asparagus and blend thoroughly with egg yolks. Then combine mixtures, simmer for 30 minutes and serve.

If fresh asparagus is not in season, try either broccoli or string beans as a substitute.

VEGETABLES

Most pediatricians believe in giving vegetables to babies when they are between eight and ten weeks old. They generally recommend feeding a baby the same vegetable for three or four consecutive days in order to detect any possible allergies to it.

Once a baby has begun to eat vegetables, there is no limit to the different kinds he may have.

String Beans

Wash and cut enough string beans into inch-lengths to fill 1/4 cup. Boil string beans in 2 inches water for 12-15 minutes.

Drain, then blend with 1/2 tablespoon soft butter, 1 teaspoon lemon juice (if baby is old enough) and serve.

To enhance your string beans, mix in one slice of cooked, crumbled bacon.

Baked Tomato

Peel and halve one medium-sized tomato. Spread top with soft butter and bake at 375° for 20 minutes. Blend lightly before serving.

For those family members over age two, add a pinch of garlic powder and Parmesan cheese.

Beets

1/4 cup fresh beets
1/2 tablespoon soft butter

Wash and slice beets finely. Cook in about 1 1/2 inches boiling water for 12 minutes or until soft. Drain water, then mash with butter.

Sometimes fresh beets taste a bit sour. If so, add a dash of sugar.

Lima Beans

Boil 1/4 cup canned or frozen lima beans in about 2 inches water until tender. Drain water, then mash with 2 teaspoons soft butter.

As a variation, mix raspberry Jell-O in with your lima beans.

Mashed Turnips

1/4 cup white turnips
1/2 tablespoon soft butter

Peel turnips and cut into half-inch slices. Boil in about 2 inches water for approximately 15 minutes or until fork goes easily through them. Drain, blend with butter and serve.

If the turnips taste sour, add 1/4 teaspoon sugar.

Peas

Boil 1/4 cup fresh peas in about 1 1/2 inches water until soft. Drain, then blend peas with 1/2 tablespoon soft butter and 1 teaspoon milk.

Raw peas in sour cream and chives make an excellent cold vegetable dish.

Artichoke Heart

Wash artichoke, cut off stem and cook in boiling water for about 45 minutes or until leaves come off easily. Remove leaves, cut out heart, mash with 1 teaspoon melted butter and serve.

Some members of your family will probably enjoy eating the leaves. For a great dip, mix 3 tablespoons melted butter with 1 tablespoon mayonnaise and 1 teaspoon garlic powder.

Corn

Boil 1/4 cup corn kernels in about 1 1/2 inches water for 12 minutes. Drain water and blend with 1 tablespoon soft butter and 1 tablespoon milk.

Blend corn with ground round steak for a nourishing meal.

Brussels Sprouts

Boil 3 Brussels sprouts in about 2 inches water for approximately 12 minutes or until soft. Blend with 2 teaspoons soft butter and serve.

If your baby is old enough to eat citrus fruit, add 1 teaspoon lime juice.

Spinach

1/2 cup fresh spinach leaves
1/2 tablespoon butter

Melt butter in a small saucepan or frying pan. Add 1/8 cup water. Spread spinach leaves over butter and water mixture. Cook for about 1 minute or until tender, blend and serve.

I believe it's a myth that most babies don't like spinach. All the babies I know eat it enthusiastically. It's only when they grow older and learn that children are not "supposed" to like spinach that they obediently turn against it.

Broccoli

1/4 cup fresh broccoli (no stems)
1/2 tablespoon butter

Boil broccoli flowerets for 15 minutes or until tender in 2 inches water. Drain broccoli, mash with soft butter and serve.

If your baby is old enough to appreciate various shapes, see what he thinks of broccoli "trees" planted in his mashed potatoes.

Asparagus

Cut tips off four asparagus stalks. Wash and boil tips in 1 1/2 inches water for 12-15 minutes. Drain water from asparagus, then mash together with 1/2 tablespoon soft butter.

Mix cold asparagus, cucumber, scallions and lettuce together for a quick but tasty salad.

Zucchini

Peel squash and cut into enough 1/8-inch slices to fill 1/4 cup. Boil in about 1 1/2 inches water until soft. Drain, then mix thoroughly in blender with 1/2 tablespoon soft butter.

For added flavor, blend in 1/4 peeled tomato.

Corn Pudding
(Serves 4)

2 eggs
2 cups fresh grated corn
2 teaspoons sugar
2 tablespoons butter
1 3/4 cups milk

Beat eggs, then add corn and sugar. Heat butter and milk together in a saucepan until butter has melted and milk is hot. Add to egg mixture, then pour into a greased baking dish. Bake at 325° for about 40 minutes until pudding is hard.

This pudding goes particularly well with chicken.

Spinach Soufflé

1/2 cup spinach
1 tablespoon butter
1 teaspoon flour
1/4 cup milk
1 egg, separated
1 tablespoon lemon juice

Cook spinach (according to recipe in this section). In a saucepan, melt butter and mix with flour. Add milk slowly. When mixture begins to thicken, add egg yolk, spinach and lemon juice. Beat egg white stiff and fold into mixture. Pour into a buttered baking dish and cook for 30 minutes.

Either leftover lamb or chicken will make an interesting addition to this soufflé.

Broccoli in Hollandaise Sauce

1/4 cup fresh broccoli (no stems)
1 tablespoon butter
1 teaspoon flour
1/8 cup milk
1/2 egg, beaten
2 teaspoons fresh lemon juice

Boil broccoli flowerets for 15 minutes or until tender in 2 inches water. While broccoli is boiling, melt butter in a small saucepan. Stir in flour. Slowly add milk, then egg and lemon juice. Drain cooked broccoli, mash and add to hollandaise-sauce mixture.

You can turn this recipe into a tempting casserole by adding 1/4 cup finely chopped cooked chicken.

Creamed Cauliflower

1/4 cup cauliflower
1/2 slice American cheese
1/2 tablespoon butter

Boil cauliflower for 12 minutes in about 2 inches water. Drain water and mash. Over low flame, melt cheese and butter over mashed cauliflower and serve.

To enhance the family's portions, sprinkle with lemon juice and mint leaves.

Cauliflower

Chop enough fresh cauliflower to fill 1/4 cup. Boil for 12 minutes or until tender in about 2 inches water. Drain cooked cauliflower, add 1/2 tablespoon soft butter, mash and serve.

Raw cauliflower makes a great hors d'oeuvre, especially when dipped into a sauce made of one part chili sauce to two parts sour cream.

Carrots

Wash and clean one small carrot. Boil in about 1½ inches water until soft. Drain water from carrot, mash with 2 teaspoons soft butter and serve.

Creamed Asparagus Tips

4 asparagus tips
1 tablespoon butter
1 teaspoon flour
1/4 cup milk
1/2 egg yolk

Cut tips off asparagus stalks. Wash and boil in 1 1/2 inches water for 12-15 minutes, until tender. Blend butter and flour together. Stir in milk and egg yolk. When mixture thickens, add asparagus tips, let simmer for a few minutes and serve.

If your baby loves eggs, sprinkle a chopped hard-boiled egg over the tips.

OMELETS

There is no limit to the different kinds of omelets you can make—fruit, vegetable, meat, cheese—they are all here! And chances are your baby will love every one.

Apricot Omelet

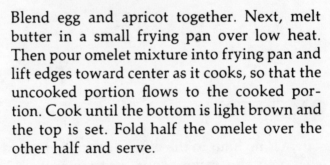

1 egg
1 fresh apricot, peeled and pitted
2 tablespoons butter

Blend egg and apricot together. Next, melt butter in a small frying pan over low heat. Then pour omelet mixture into frying pan and lift edges toward center as it cooks, so that the uncooked portion flows to the cooked portion. Cook until the bottom is light brown and the top is set. Fold half the omelet over the other half and serve.

Don't be surprised if the other members of your family love Apricot Omelet as much as your baby does!

Ham and Cheese Omelet

1/8 cup finely chopped cooked ham
1 egg
1/8 cup grated Swiss cheese
2 tablespoons butter

Blend egg, cheese and ham together. Melt butter in a small frying pan over low heat. Pour omelet into frying pan and lift edges toward center as it cooks, so that the uncooked portion flows to the cooked portion. Cook until the bottom is light brown and the top is set. Fold half the omelet over the other half and serve.

The rest of you may enjoy this omelet between two slices of French toast.

Lima Bean Omelet

1/4 cup cooked lima beans
1 egg
2 tablespoons butter

Beat egg and blend with lima beans. Heat butter in a small frying pan over low heat until it has melted. Pour omelet into frying pan and lift edges toward center as it cooks, so that the uncooked portion flows to the cooked portion. Cook until the bottom is light brown and the top is set. Fold half the omelet over the other half and serve.

You can make a savory variation of this dish by adding 1/8 cup corn and several slices of cooked, finely crumbled bacon to the omelet mixture.

Spinach Omelet

1/4 cup fresh cooked spinach
1 egg
1/8 cup milk
2 tablespoons butter

Blend spinach, egg and milk together. Melt butter in a small frying pan over low heat. Pour omelet into frying pan. Lift edges toward the center as it cooks to let the uncooked portion flow to the cooked portion. Cook until the bottom is light brown and the top is set. Fold half the omelet over the other half and serve.

If you're going to make this for the "over-two" members of your family, spice it up with nutmeg and chives.

Bacon and Potato Omelet

1/2 small potato
1 slice cooked bacon
2 tablespoons butter
1 egg

Peel potato and dice finely. Use a small frying pan to sauté potatoes in 1 tablespoon butter. Crumble bacon finely and beat with egg. Put 1 tablespoon butter on top of sautéed potatoes, then pour egg mixture over them. Cook over low heat. As the omelet cooks, lift the edges toward center so uncooked mixture flows to cooked mixture. Cook until bottom is light brown and top is set. Fold half the omelet over the other half and serve.

If you are not serving a sugary dessert, make this omelet a very special treat by adding 1 teaspoon maple syrup.

MEAT

Usually babies begin to eat meat when they
are between 12 and 14 weeks old. Most pediatricians recommend beef, lamb, veal, pork and
ham. The U.S. Department of ·Agriculture
grades the quality of beef, lamb and veal as
follows: prime (the very finest), choice (high
quality, the best buy), good (fair quality),
commercial and utility. The latter two are not
recommended for home use and are rarely
found in supermarkets. Pork and ham show
fewer differences in quality and therefore
fewer grades.

Beef Stew

1/4 cup ground round steak
4 string beans
1/4 tomato, peeled
1/2 boiled potato

Broil ground round steak. Place in blender with cooked string beans (see recipe in the vegetable section) and tomato. Mix and pour into a casserole dish. Dice boiled potato and sprinkle over top. Bake for 15 minutes at 350°.

Either lamb or pot roast makes a perfect meat substitute.

Ground Round Steak

Shape 1/4 cup ground round steak into a patty and broil. For extra smoothness, use blender.

If you are pressed for time, remember that ground round steak is particularly quick and easy to prepare.

Meatballs and Gravy

1/4 cup ground round steak
1 tablespoon butter
1 teaspoon flour
1/4 cup milk

Shape ground round steak into tiny meatballs. Broil in a pan greased lightly with butter. Blend butter and flour together over low heat. Add milk and stir. When mixture begins to thicken add juice from cooked meat and let simmer for about a minute. Pour gravy over meatballs.

This is even more nourishing served on toast.

Beef-Bacon Puffs

1/4 cup ground round steak
2-3 slices cooked bacon

Roll ground round steak into little puffs and broil. Wrap a bacon slice around each puff and serve.

Beef-Bacon Puffs also make scrumptious-tasting hot hors d'oeuvres.

Meat Loaf

1/4 cup cooked ground round steak
1/2 tomato, peeled
1/8 cup grated American cheese
1/2 egg, beaten
1/8 cup finely crumbled arrowroot
   cookies

Blend ground round steak, tomato, cheese,

egg and arrowroot cookies for 10-12 seconds. Pour mixture into a greased baking dish and bake at 375° for 35 minutes.

If Meat Loaf becomes one of your baby's favorite dishes, you can save yourself time in the kitchen by doubling the recipe and serving cold meat loaf the following day for lunch.

Lamb Chop

Broil a medium-sized lamb chop and cut off 1/4 cup meat. Blend meat thoroughly with 1/2 tablespoon soft butter and 1/8 cup plus 2 tablespoons water.

To round out the meal, serve Sweet Potato (see recipe in potato section) and String Beans (see recipe in vegetable section) with the lamb chop.

Leg of Lamb

Blend thoroughly 1/4 cup cooked lamb with 1/8 cup plus 2 tablespoons water.

Garnish your family's lamb portions with heated strawberry jam and mint leaves.

Lamb and Gravy

1/4 cup baked lamb
1 tablespoon butter
1 teaspoon flour
1/4 cup milk
1/4 cup juice from lamb

Blend 1/4 cup lamb thoroughly with 1/8 cup plus 2 tablespoons water. Mix butter and flour together in a pan over low heat. Add milk and stir. When mixture begins to thicken add juice from lamb. Then pour thickened gravy over lamb.

If you like to bake your lamb in a sauce, ask

your butcher to cut off a portion for the baby. Pop his serving into the oven about 15 minutes before yours is ready.

Apricot-Lamb Combo

1 lamb chop
1 apricot

Broil lamb chop. Cut off 1/4 cup meat and blend thoroughly with 1/4 cup water. Then add peeled, pitted apricot, blend and serve.

Spinach Soufflé is a fine complement to this combination.

Ham

Blend thoroughly 1/4 cup cooked ham with 1/8 cup plus 2 tablespoons water.

If you're baking a ham rather than using ready-cooked slices, keep it moist and juicy by frosting the top with crushed pineapple.

Ham Splurge

1/4 cup finely diced cooked ham
1/8 cup crushed pineapple
1/2 small mashed sweet potato
1/2 tablespoon butter

Mash ham and pineapple together with sweet potato (cooked according to recipe in potato section). Top with butter. Cook in a greased baking dish at 350° for 20 minutes before serving.

If your baby is at the cheese age, try sprinkling grated Swiss cheese over the Ham Splurge.

Ham and Egg

1/4 cup cooked ham
1 egg
1/8 cup milk

Blend ham thoroughly with 1/8 cup plus 2 tablespoons water. Beat egg in bowl and add milk. In a lightly greased frying pan, scramble ham and egg mixture together.

For the noninfants in your family, serve a larger portion of this dish with cinnamon sprinkled generously over the top.

Ham and Yams

1/4 cup cooked ham
1/4 cup yams (frozen, canned or fresh
but without candied syrup)
1/2 tablespoon soft butter

Blend ham thoroughly with 1/8 cup plus 2 tablespoons water. Heat yams until warm and soft, then blend with butter and serve.

The adults will probably enjoy brown sugar sprinkled over their yams.

Ham and Spinach Soufflé

1/4 cup finely diced cooked ham
1/2 cup spinach
1 tablespoon butter
1 teaspoon flour
1/4 cup milk
1 egg, separated

Cook spinach (according to recipe in vegetable section). In a saucepan, melt butter, then add flour and stir. Blend in milk and egg yolk. When mixture begins to thicken, stir in spinach and ham. Beat egg white until stiff and fold into mixture. Pour into a buttered soufflé dish and cook for about 30 minutes at 350°.

For those who appreciate curry, serve Ham and Spinach Soufflé with hot curried fruit. Pour canned mixed fruit into a baking dish with 1 teaspoon curry for each 6-ounce can, sprinkle brown sugar over the top and bake for 30 minutes at 350°.

Ham-Peach Combo

1/4 cup cooked ham
1 small peach, peeled and pitted
1/8 cup milk

Blend ham, peach and milk until smooth.
If fresh peaches are out of season, pineapple
or pear can be substituted.

Pork in Apple Cider

1/4 cup finely chopped cooked pork
1/8 cup plus 2 tablespoons apple
  cider

Blend pork and apple cider together, heat and
serve.

If you don't have apple cider on hand, use
apple or pineapple juice instead.

49

Pork Chop

Broil one pork chop until no pink meat is in evidence. Cut off 1/4 cup meat and blend with 1/8 cup plus two tablespoons water.

When you are preparing any pork dish for your baby and for your family, make certain the meat is so thoroughly cooked that no trace of pinkness remains.

Pork à l'Orange

1/4 cup finely chopped cooked pork
1/8 cup orange juice
1 tablespoon orange marmalade

Blend pork, orange juice and orange marmalade together, heat and serve.

String beans and rice combine nicely with Pork à l'Orange.

Pork Goulash

1/4 cup cooked pork
1/2 sweet potato
1/4 cup milk
3 string beans
1/3 carrot

Blend pork with cooked sweet potato (see recipe in potato section) and milk. Cook string beans and carrot (see recipes in vegetable section). Heat mixtures together in a saucepan and serve.

If you make this dish often, substitute other vegetables such as peas and beets or lima beans and tomato.

Pork and Macaroni

Pork

Blend 1/4 cup cooked pork with 1/8 cup plus 2 tablespoons water. Stir pork into macaroni and serve.

Macaroni

Cook 1/4 cup macaroni in boiling water until soft. Drain. In another pan, melt 1/8 cup American cheese with 1/4 cup milk and one egg yolk. When cheese has melted, add cooked noodles and stir.

To round out the meal, serve Apple Tapioca for dessert.

Scrambled Veal and Egg

1 veal cutlet
1 tablespoon butter
1 egg
1/8 cup milk

Broil veal cutlet. Cut off 1/4 cup meat and blend thoroughly with butter and 3 tablespoons water. Beat egg in a bowl. Add milk and veal to egg, then scramble in a lightly buttered frying pan.

To bring out the best flavor in this dish cook slowly over low heat and serve slightly moist.

Veal-Stuffed Tomato

1/4 cup chopped cooked veal
1/8 cup milk
1 egg yolk
1/2 tomato
1/2 tablespoon butter
1 arrowroot cookie

Blend veal (roasted or broiled) with milk, egg yolk, and scooped center of tomato. Pour mixture into 1/2 tomato shell, placed in a greased baking dish. Surround shell with leftover mixture. Place butter on top of tomato-shell mixture. Sprinkle arrowroot cookie crumbs over top. Bake at 375° for 15 minutes.

Veal-Stuffed Tomatoes make great hors d'oeuvres. Substitute cherry tomatoes for the regular-sized ones.

Veal Pancake

1 veal cutlet
1/8 cup flour
1/2 egg
1/4 cup milk
1/2 carrot

Broil veal cutlet. Cut off 1/4 cup meat and blend thoroughly with 1/8 cup plus 2 tablespoons water. In a bowl, mix flour with beaten egg and milk. Pour batter into a lightly buttered frying pan. When pancake is ready, spread veal mixture and carrot (see recipe in vegetable section) onto pancake. Roll and serve.

You may want to vary this recipe by substituting 1/4 apple (as prepared in the fruit section) for the carrot.

Veal Cutlet

1 veal cutlet
1/8 cup flour
1/2 egg
1 tablespoon lemon juice

Roll veal cutlet in flour, then shake off excess. Dip into beaten egg. Grease a frying pan with butter and brown cutlet for about 3 minutes on each side, until cooked. Cut off 1/4 cup meat, blend thoroughly with lemon juice and 1/8 cup plus 2 tablespoons water and serve.

When you're preparing veal cutlets for the more seasoned eaters, add 1 teaspoon garlic powder and 1 tablespoon grated Swiss cheese to each cutlet.

Veal and Tater Pie

1 veal cutlet
1/8 cup flour
1/2 egg
1/4 tomato, peeled
1/4 cup mashed potatoes

Roll veal cutlet in flour. Shake off excess. Dip into beaten egg and broil. Cut off 1/4 cup meat and blend thoroughly with 1/8 cup plus 2 tablespoons water. Pour into a baking dish. Then blend tomato and pour over meat mixture. Frost top with mashed potatoes (see recipe in potato section), cook for 20 minutes at 325° and serve.

For a light dessert to offset this rich meal, serve Peach Surprise.

POULTRY

By the time they are 12 to 14 weeks old most babies are beginning to eat chicken and turkey.

You'll find lots of good, hearty recipes to choose from in this section. A soufflé, a casserole, you name it! And look for more poultry recipes in the International Section.

Club Chicken

1/4 cup finely diced cooked chicken
1/8 cup finely diced cooked ham
1/2 tomato, peeled
1 slice cooked bacon, finely chopped

Arrange chicken and ham in layers in a greased baking dish. Blend tomato, then pour over chicken and ham. Sprinkle bacon over top and bake at 350° for 25 minutes.

While you've got the ingredients on hand, why not make club sandwiches for the rest of the family?

Chicken Casserole

1/4 cup finely diced cooked chicken
1/8 cup peas
1/4 tomato, peeled
1 arrowroot cookie

Cook peas (see recipe in vegetable section), then blend with chicken and tomato. Pour into a lightly greased baking dish and crumble arrowroot cookie over top. Bake for 20 minutes at 375° and serve.

Fruit soup nicely complements this casserole.

Chicken

Blend 1/4 cup cooked chicken with 1/8 cup plus 2 tablespoons water and serve.

As your baby grows older, he'll enjoy his own special stuffing, made with 1/2 cup bread crumbs, 1/8 cup finely chopped celery, 1 egg yolk and 1/8 cup milk. Cook it in the smaller opening of the chicken to leave room in the larger opening for your "grown-up" stuffing recipe.

Creamed Chicken

1/4 cup cooked chicken
1 teaspoon flour
1 tablespoon butter
1/4 cup milk

Blend flour and butter in a pan over low heat. Add milk and stir. When mixture begins to thicken, add chicken, let simmer for several minutes and serve.

If your baby's first birthday party includes lunch or dinner, this is an excellent dish to serve, either in a patty shell, over mashed potatoes or on toast.

Chicken Soufflé

1/4 cup finely diced cooked chicken
1 teaspoon flour
1 tablespoon butter
1/4 cup milk
1 egg yolk, beaten

Blend flour and butter in a pan over low heat. Add milk and stir. When mixture begins to thicken add egg yolk and chicken. Let simmer for a minute before pouring into a lightly greased baking dish. Bake for 35 minutes at 350°.

To vary this recipe, add a fruit—1/8 cup pear or peach—or a vegetable—1/8 cup broccoli or spinach.

Turkey

Blend 1/4 cup cooked turkey with 1/8 cup plus 2 tablespoons water and serve.

You need not restrict turkey dinners to Thanksgiving and Christmas. There are 3 to 6 pound turkeys available at most markets throughout the year.

Turkey Special

1/4 cup cooked turkey
1/4 cup sweet potato
1/8 cup string beans

Blend turkey with 1/8 cup plus 2 tablespoons water. Prepare sweet potato (according to recipe in potato section) and string beans (according to recipe in vegetable section). Serve in combination or alternate 1 spoonful of each.

Here's a fine recipe with which to introduce your baby to cranberry jelly.

Creamed Turkey on Potato

1/4 cup cooked turkey
1 tablespoon butter
1 teaspoon flour
1/4 cup milk
1/4 cup mashed or baked potato

Blend turkey with 1/8 cup plus 2 tablespoons water. Combine butter and flour in a pan over low heat. Add milk and stir. When mixture thickens add turkey. Then pour over potato (see recipes in potato section).

If you're short on time, you can serve this on toast.

Turkey-Noodle Casserole

1/4 cup finely chopped cooked turkey
1/8 cup egg noodles
1 tablespoon butter
1 teaspoon flour
1/4 cup milk
1/8 cup zucchini with tomato

Cook noodles in boiling water until soft. Drain, then blend with turkey and 1 tablespoon water. Mix butter and flour together over low heat. Add milk and stir. When mixture begins to thicken add turkey, noodles and zucchini with tomato (cooked according to recipe in vegetable section). Pour mixture into a casserole dish, bake for about 20 minutes at 350°.

This is a perfect casserole to make with roast turkey leftovers.

FISH

Babies usually begin to eat fish when they are between twelve and fourteen weeks old. However, some pediatricians believe that mothers should wait until their baby is at least ten months old before introducing fish into the diet.

Many of the recipes in this section call for fillet of sole because this cut of fish has few, if any, bones. But it is still necessary to comb through the fish to make sure that no bones remain.

Poached Tomato Sole

Blend a small piece of cooked fillet of sole with 1/2 medium-sized tomato. Place in a lightly greased baking dish, then set dish in a shallow pan of water. Bake for about 10 minutes at 350°.

If you're poaching sole for the rest of the family, pour 1/8 cup hot brandy over each portion.

Fish Stew

Blend a small piece of cooked fillet of sole with 1/4 cup milk, 1/2 boiled potato, 1 small cooked carrot and 4 string beans (see recipes in vegetable section). Pour into a lightly greased baking dish and bake at 325° for 12-15 minutes.

If you wish, substitute 1/4 cup cooked rice or macaroni (cooked according to recipe in meat section) for the potato.

Fillet of Sole with Rice

Place a small piece of fillet of sole in a lightly greased baking dish. Melt 1/4 cup butter. Blend with 1/4 cup milk and pour over sole. Bake at 350° until tender.

Cook 1/4 cup rice according to directions on package. Blend fish and rice before serving.

Try serving Fillet of Sole for breakfast. Many adults eat fish in the morning and there's no reason babies can't either.

Mousse of Sole

Blend a small piece of cooked fillet of sole with 1 egg white and 1/8 cup milk. Pour into a buttered baking dish. Cover with aluminum foil, then place dish in a shallow pan of water. Bake until firm, about 20-30 minutes.

Mousse of Sole is particularly good seasoned with a sprinkling of lemon or lime juice.

Creamed Fish on Banana Bread

Bake Banana Bread (according to recipe in the bread section). Pour a beaten egg over a small piece of fillet of sole, and broil for about 12 minutes, until tender, in a lightly greased pan. Then blend fish. Melt 1 tablespoon butter with 1 teaspoon flour in a saucepan over low heat. Pour in 1/4 cup milk and when mixture begins to thicken, add fish. Pour fish mixture over a slice of Banana Bread.

Many babies seem to favor Creamed Fish on Applesauce Bread (see recipe in bread section).

Tuna-Avocado Salad

1/8 cup finely chopped tuna
1/8 cup mashed avocado
2 teaspoons mayonnaise

Blend tuna, avocado (as prepared in fruit section) and mayonnaise together thoroughly and serve.

It is important to use only ripe avocados as the unripe are almost impossible to mash or blend.

Creamed Tuna over Corn Bread

1/4 cup finely chopped tuna
1 tablespoon butter
1 teaspoon flour
1/3 cup milk

Melt butter in a saucepan. Mix flour with butter and add milk. When mixture begins to thicken stir in tuna and let simmer for a few minutes before pouring over a slice of Corn Bread (baked according to recipe in bread section).

Creamed tuna is a well known favorite served on toast as well as over rice or mashed potatoes.

Creamed Tuna and Egg with Asparagus

1/4 cup finely chopped tuna
1 tablespoon butter
1 teaspoon flour
1/2 cup milk
2 cooked asparagus tips
1/4 finely chopped hard-boiled egg

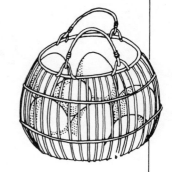

Melt butter in a saucepan. Mix flour with butter, then add milk. When mixture begins to thicken stir in tuna, asparagus (see recipe in vegetable section) and hard-boiled egg. Let simmer for a few minutes. Then blend, reheat and serve.

This dish is particularly filling and therefore ideal for babies with big appetites.

Tuna-Artichoke Casserole

1/4 cup tuna
1/8 cup plus 2 tablespoons milk
1 artichoke heart, cooked
2 teaspoons soft butter
1 graham cracker, finely crumbled

Blend tuna, milk, artichoke heart (see recipe in vegetable section), butter and graham cracker crumbs together. Place in a lightly greased baking dish and bake at 350° for about 20 minutes.

For a change of pace, substitute 1/8 cup finely crumbled cornflakes for the graham cracker.

INTERNATIONAL DISHES

A twelve-week-old baby is old enough to eat
Cassoulet of Lamb and Pineapple Chicken.
And a baby doesn't need to be much older to
enjoy many other international favorites as
well.

Osso Buco

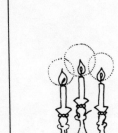

1/4 cup cooked veal
1 slice cooked bacon
1/8 cup cooked carrots
1/2 tomato, peeled
1 tablespoon butter
1/2 tablespoon flour
1 beef bouillon cube
1/8 cup plus 2 tablespoons milk

Blend veal, bacon, carrots (see recipe in vegetable section) and tomato. In a small saucepan melt butter, then add flour and bouillon cube. When mixture thickens, add milk, stir until smooth. Pour veal mixture into a heated serving dish (or heat briefly in a saucepan). Pour gravy over veal and serve.

To give your baby an extra special treat, serve Orange Soufflé for dessert.

Cassoulet of Lamb

1/4 cup cooked lamb
1/8 cup milk
1/4 tomato, peeled
1 slice bacon
1/3 medium-sized carrot
3 string beans

Blend the lamb thoroughly with milk and tomato, then pour into a greased casserole dish. Fry bacon. Cook carrot and string beans (according to recipes in vegetable section). Blend vegetables thoroughly before adding to casserole dish. Crumble bacon very finely, then sprinkle over top. Bake for about 25 minutes at 350°.

For an especially tasty variation of this dish, use 1/8 cup baked beans in place of string beans.

Mexican Plate

Taco

1/4 cup ground round steak
1/2 tablespoon soft butter
1/8 cup finely diced tomato
1/8 cup grated American cheese

Broil ground round steak. Blend with butter, tomato and cheese. Heat and serve with Guacamole.

Guacamole

Mash 1/4 avocado with 1 tablespoon lemon juice and serve.

Tacos and Guacamole are traditional favorites south of the border and they'll make a tasty as well as nourishing meal for your baby.

Spaghetti and Meat Sauce

1/3 cup spaghetti noodles
1/4 cup ground round steak
1 small tomato, peeled
1 tablespoon butter
1 teaspoon flour
1/4 cup milk

Boil noodles for about 12 minutes, until soft, and drain. Meanwhile, broil ground round steak and blend with tomato. Melt butter in a saucepan, then add flour. When the mixture begins to thicken, add milk and stir. Pour in meat sauce, let simmer for 5 minutes and serve over noodles.

If your baby is overweight, it's a good idea to substitute skim milk.

Italian Chicken

1/4 cup fresh cooked chicken
1/8 cup milk
1 tablespoon butter
1 slice American cheese
1/2 tomato, peeled

Blend milk, butter, cheese and tomato in a double boiler. When cheese has melted add chicken (which has been either finely diced or blended with 1/8 cup water) and serve.

If you have the time, bake some Italian Bread (see recipe in the bread section) to accompany this dish.

Swiss Egg Treat

1 egg
1/4 tomato, peeled
1/8 cup grated Swiss cheese
3 tablespoons milk
1 teaspoon butter

Blend egg, tomato, cheese and milk together. Melt butter in a small frying pan, then scramble egg mixture over low heat.

Swiss Egg Treat is even better served on toast spread with apricot (as prepared in fruit section).

Quiche Lorraine
(Serves 4)

Pastry Crust
1 1/3 cups flour
1/2 teaspoon baking powder
1/4 cup sugar
1 egg
1 teaspoon vanilla
2 tablespoons butter

Sift flour, baking powder and sugar together.
Mix with egg and vanilla. Knead ingredients
together until thick and smooth. If necessary,
add a few drops of water. Sprinkle flour over
bottom of 10-inch round baking dish. Spread

crust evenly around baking dish. Dab small pats of butter over crust.

Filling
5 eggs
2 tablespoons flour
1 3/4 cups milk
10 slices cooked, crumbled bacon
2 cups grated Swiss cheese

Blend eggs, flour and milk. Stir in bacon and cheese. Pour into baking dish over pastry crust. Bake at 400° for about 40 minutes, cut into wedges, and serve.

You can substitute 1/2 cup finely diced ham for the bacon or combine the two, using 5 slices bacon and 1/4 cup ham.

Pineapple Chicken

1/4 cup finely diced cooked chicken
1/8 cup crushed (or mashed) fresh
 pineapple
1/2 tablespoon butter

Melt butter in a small saucepan. Add chicken
and pineapple. Blend together until warm and
serve.

Egg noodles and snow peas served with
Pineapple Chicken transform this into a su-
perb Chinese treat.

POTATOES

I can remember the days when most babies had to wait until they were a year old before they were given potatoes. Now most pediatricians consider 8-to-10 weeks old a suitable time to feed a baby potatoes as long as they are of a smooth consistency.

Baked Potato

Wash a small potato thoroughly. Bake for about 30 minutes at 450° or until fork goes through the center easily. Cut down middle and mash 1/2 tablespoon soft butter throughout.

See if your baby likes finely chopped meat mixed in with his baked potato.

Mashed Potato

Peel a small potato. Boil until soft. Mash together with 1 tablespoon soft butter and 2 tablespoons milk.

If you have some extra time and you are in a creative mood, form the mashed potato into a particular shape—a snowman, flower, star.

Stuffed Baked Potato

Scrub a small potato well, then bake at 450° for about 30 minutes or until fork goes easily through center. Then cut in half, scoop potato from skin and mash. Mix in 1 teaspoon milk and 1 teaspoon butter. Refill shells, reheat at 350° for about 10 minutes and serve.

If your baby can eat cheese, sprinkle 1 teaspoon grated Parmesan cheese over his potato.

Mashed Sweet Potato

Peel a small sweet potato. Boil until soft. Mash together with 1 tablespoon soft butter, 1 tablespoon milk and serve.

The grown-ups may prefer sherry in place of the milk.

Potato Salad
(Serves 4-6)

4 potatoes
2 hard-boiled eggs
2 slices finely crumbled cooked bacon
1/3 cup pickle relish juice
3/4 cup mayonnaise

Peel potatoes and cut into half-inch slices. Boil for about 25 minutes or until fork goes easily through them. Drain water from potatoes and blend them with eggs, bacon, relish juice and mayonnaise.

Season the adults' portions with 1/2 teaspoon onion powder.

Baked Sweet Potato

Wash a small sweet potato thoroughly. Bake for about 35 minutes at 450° or until a fork goes through it easily. Cut down middle, mash 1/2 tablespoon soft butter throughout and serve.

Believe it or not, I know a baby who eats his sweet potato combined with applesauce and vanilla ice cream!

Potatoes au Gratin

1/2 medium-sized potato
1 tablespoon butter
1/4 cup milk
1/8 cup grated Parmesan cheese

Peel and cut potato into thin slices. Place in a greased baking dish. Dab a small pat of butter on each slice of potato. Pour milk and sprinkle cheese over potatoes. Bake at 400° for about 12 minutes or until slices are tender.

The older children in your family may go wild over gratinburgers—a broiled hamburger patty topped with a layer of potatoes au gratin and french fried onion rings.

BREADS

Most people think of baking bread as a long, involved process, but for most kinds of bread this is no longer the case.

Although you won't find the typical breads in this section, there are six different kinds your baby as well as the other members in your family should enjoy.

Peanut Butter Bread
(1 loaf)

1 3/4 cups all-purpose flour
1/3 cup sugar
1 3/4 teaspoons baking powder
3/4 cup peanut butter
1 cup plus 1 tablespoon milk

Sift flour, sugar and baking powder together. Blend with peanut butter. Stir in milk and spoon the mixture into a buttered bread pan. Bake at 350° for about 45 minutes.

Jelly or jam makes a great spread over this bread.

Banana Bread
(1 loaf)

4 small bananas
1 cup sugar
1 large egg
1 1/2 cups plus 2 tablespoons sifted
   flour
1/3 cup melted butter
3/4 teaspoon baking soda

Mash bananas. Blend in sugar, egg, flour, butter and baking soda. Pour into a lightly greased bread pan and bake for 1 hour at 325°.

This bread tastes best served warm.

Applesauce Bread
(1 loaf)

1 cup applesauce
3/4 cup sugar
1 egg, beaten
2 tablespoons melted butter
1 1/4 cups sifted flour
1 teaspoon baking soda

Blend applesauce with sugar, egg, butter, flour and baking soda. Pour into a lightly greased bread pan and bake for 1 hour at 325°.

To give this bread an even fruitier flavor, add a fresh peach, pear or apricot (as prepared in the fruit section).

Oatmeal Bread
(2 loaves)

1 package yeast
2 1/2 cups boiling water
3/4 cup rolled oats
1/2 cup molasses
3 tablespoons melted butter
4 1/3 cups sifted flour

Dissolve yeast in 1/2 cup boiling water.

Blend 2 cups boiling water with oats, molasses, butter and the dissolved yeast. Add flour and let rise until it has almost doubled in size. Then bake in greased bread pans at 350° for about 55 minutes.

Strawberry jelly makes this bread even tastier.

Italian Bread
(2 loaves)

1 package yeast
1 cup plus 2 tablespoons warm water
2 tablespoons sugar
2 tablespoons shortening
2 cups plus one tablespoon flour
1 egg white, beaten

In a large mixing bowl blend yeast and water together. Let stand for five minutes. Then add sugar, shortening and flour.

Sprinkle a board with flour. Knead dough well and shape into long slender loaves. Place loaves on cookie sheets and cut diagonal slits about 1/4 inch deep across each surface. Brush 1/2 egg white over tops of loaves. Bake at 425° for 10 minutes. Then brush remaining egg white over top and bake for 25 minutes at 375°. (Bake with a large pan of boiling water in the oven under the rack where bread is placed.)

If you want to please the garlic lovers in your family, cut one loaf into 1 1/2-inch slices. Melt 1/2 cup butter and blend with 3 tablespoons garlic powder. Soak each slice with garlic mixture and heat in oven.

Corn Bread
(Serves 4-6)

3/4 cup sifted flour
1 tablespoon baking powder
3 tablespoons sugar
2/3 cup yellow cornmeal
2 eggs
3/4 cup plus 1 tablespoon milk
1/3 cup melted butter

Mix flour, baking powder, sugar and cornmeal together. Beat eggs and mix with milk and butter. Blend the liquid and dry ingredients together and pour into an 8-inch greased pan. Bake at 400° for about 30 minutes.

If you're baking Corn Bread during the various holiday seasons, use appropriate molds. It's an amusing way to add to your baby's eating enjoyment.

DESSERTS

There's everything from a simple fruit dessert to chocolate mousse in this section.

Naturally the richer, more sugary desserts should be saved for occasional treats. But there are many others that are so healthy and nourishing they can be eaten even at break-fast.

Apricot Treat

Remove pit from apricot. Peel, then blend thoroughly with 1/8 cup water. Pour into a serving dish and crumble a graham cracker over the top.

If you have butter cookies or brownies on hand, either can be substituted for the graham cracker.

Peach Surprise

Peel and remove pit from a fresh, ripe peach. Blend and pour into a serving dish. Frost top with pablum. Sprinkle lightly with sugar and serve.

If your baby does not finish his bottle, pour the rest of the milk over his Peach Surprise.

Sweet Banana

Peel a banana. Mash half, pour milk over top and sprinkle lightly with sugar.

Sweet Banana as well as Apricot Treat and Peach Surprise are great breakfast desserts.

Blueberry Splurge

12 blueberries
1/2 teaspoon sugar
1/8 cup milk

Remove stems and wash blueberries thoroughly. Blend with sugar and milk and serve.

If you prefer, use brown sugar.

Apple Tapioca

3 cups apples, sliced, peeled and cored
2/3 cup sugar
1/3 cup plus 1 tablespoon quick tapioca

Mix apples and 1/3 cup sugar together. Bake for 15 minutes at 350° in a greased baking dish. In the meantime, cook tapioca in a saucepan with 2 cups water and 1/3 cup sugar for 5 to 8 minutes (until tapioca is transparent). Pour over apples and continue baking for about 30 minutes, until apples are tender.

Pear Tapioca makes a delicious variation.

Pineapple Milk Shake

1/8 cup fresh pineapple, crushed
1/2 cup milk
1 scoop pineapple sherbet

Blend pineapple, milk and sherbet together and serve.

You can vary this basic milk-shake recipe by using any fruit and sherbet.

Orange Soufflé
(Serves 4)

4 eggs
1/3 cup sugar
2 oranges

Separate eggs. Beat whites until stiff, then blend in sugar. Beat yolks and add to mixture. Squeeze juice from oranges and stir gently into mixture. Pour into a lightly greased baking dish and bake for 40 minutes at 325°.

For the adults at your table, pour a half jigger of Grand Marnier over the top of their Orange Soufflé.

Applesauce-Jell-O Combo

Make your baby's favorite-flavored Jell-O according to directions on the package.

Peel and scoop seeds out of 1/4 apple. Blend thoroughly with 1/8 cup water and 2 teaspoons sugar. Add one serving thickened Jell-O to apple mixture, blend for about 10 seconds and serve.

Blend some fresh fruit (prepared according to the recipes in the fruit section) into the remaining Jell-O, and you'll have a quick Jell-O fruit salad for your baby.

Raspberry Slush

6 raspberries
3 generous tablespoons raspberry sherbet

Wash raspberries thoroughly. Blend with raspberry sherbet and serve.

To make all kinds of slushes, substitute various fruits and sherbets.

Chocolate Chip Cookies
(Serves 4)

1/2 cup soft butter
1/2 cup granulated sugar
1/2 cup brown sugar
1/2 egg, beaten
1 cup sifted flour
1/2 teaspoon baking soda
1 cup semisweet chocolate bits

Mix butter together with granulated and brown sugars, egg, flour and baking soda. Add chocolate bits and drop from a teaspoon onto a cookie sheet greased with butter. Bake for about 10 minutes at 375°.

Occasionally, you may want to substitute raisins for the chocolate bits.

Bananas and Junket

Make your baby's favorite-flavored junket according to directions on back of the package. Frost with 1/3 mashed banana.

If you're having a dinner party and need a simple but superb-tasting dessert, try Bananas and Junket with whipped cream, ground walnuts and Grand Marnier.

Chocolate Mousse
(Serves 4)

6 ounces semisweet chocolate
1 tablespoon orange juice
2 egg yolks
1/2 cup sugar
1 cup milk

Melt chocolate over low heat. Let cool. Blend orange juice, egg yolks, sugar and milk together. Add chocolate to this mixture and blend until smooth. Pour into individual serving dishes and refrigerate.

If any members of your family are on diets and can't resist Chocolate Mousse, substitute skim milk.

Banana Mousse
(Serves 4)

4 bananas
3 egg yolks
3 tablespoons sugar
1 cup milk

Blend bananas, egg yolks, sugar and milk together. Heat to boiling point in a saucepan. Pour into serving dishes and refrigerate about 4 hours, until firm.

For a special treat, try topping the adults' servings with a mound of fresh whipped cream and a generous amount of crème de cacao.

Brownies
(Serves 4-6)

1/2 cup soft butter
1 3/4 cups sugar
3 eggs
2/3 cup sifted flour
2 squares unsweetened chocolate

In a mixing bowl, blend butter and sugar together. Then add eggs and flour. Melt chocolate in top of a double boiler. Let cool for several minutes before pouring into mixing bowl. Blend all ingredients. Grease a baking pan with butter and pour mixture into pan. Bake for about 35 minutes at 350°.

Make sure to keep your brownies covered; otherwise they may lose their freshness before the day is over.

Custard Supreme
(Serves 4)

3 cups milk
6 egg yolks
6 tablespoons granulated sugar
2/3 cup brown sugar

Heat milk in top of a double boiler. Beat egg yolks in a mixing bowl. Stir in granulated and brown sugars. Add the warm milk slowly to egg mixture, stirring constantly. Pour mixture back into top of double boiler and cook, stirring constantly until custard coats a metal spoon. Pour custard into serving dishes and chill.

For the dieters in your family, substitute skim milk.

Butter Cookies
(Serves 4)

1/2 cup soft butter
1 cup granulated sugar
1 egg
3/4 cup sifted flour
1/2 teaspoon baking soda

Mix butter together with sugar, egg, flour and baking soda. Drop from a teaspoon onto a cookie sheet greased with butter. Bake for about 12 minutes at 350°.

It's simple to make funny faces on these cookies. Smooth out the batter with the edge of a knife and draw lines with your fingers, a pin or the point of a knitting needle.

INDEX

119